Longings Of Landour

Longings Of Landour

OrangeBooks Publication

Smriti Nagar, Bhilai, Chhattisgarh - 490020

Website: **www.orangebooks.in**

First Edition, 2022

ISBN: 978-93-5621-007-3

LONGINGS OF LANDOUR

Raghav A. Bijalwan

Raj A Bijalwan

OrangeBooks Publication

www.orangebooks.in

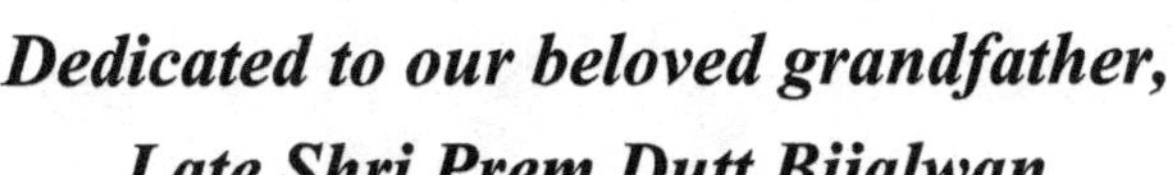

Dedicated to our beloved grandfather,
Late Shri Prem Dutt Bijalwan

Preface

Mussoorie, the Queen of Hills has been a place of historic significance. Landour is a British era cantonment and much of it continues to be a cantonment even today. Landour and Mussoorie are often considered as the twin towns. Through the portals of time, India has evolved and with it has evolved our town. This evolution has almost erased the boundaries of Mussoorie and Landour. Both Mussoorie and Landour have been a witness to the changing India, its Independence and the creation of Uttarakhand state. However, holding a historical significance doesn't ensure a sustained glory and today's Mussoorie bears the testimony of this very fact.

Through our poetries, we have echoed the longings, the dreams, the desires of the people who lived and died here only to see the town suffering. Longings of Landour presents a journey of how Landour has evolved and what exactly remains for the future. No, the poems have not been written in a melancholic tone/ mood but have merely identified the glorious past of our town that has ruined with time. There isn't any wailing but the pain has been asserted. The Queen is subtly losing the gems from its crown but no one is conscious. The budding poets have established a juncture for the readers to learn from the past and realise in order to ensure a better future of the town. Of course, development of Mussoorie is necessary but definitely not at the cost of its glory and heritage. A lot has changed as it does but through these poems we underline how step by step the town is being ruined keeping aside the very thought of a sustainable development. By sustainable development, we mean a development that keeps the glory and heritage of the town alive.

The title is Longings of Landour but the poems certainly echo the voice of the Queen of Hills. These are longings from landour for Mussoorie. The poems underline the universal law of nature: change! But this change should be a progressive one. In fact, these poems will take the readers on a tour to Mussoorie and clearly identify the forces that are solely responsible for the present condition of Mussoorie. Through the longings of Landour, we have made an attempt to revisit the past and understand what exactly made Mussoorie glorious then! Look at how changes have taken place here: big cars over long walks, chaos over silence, money over peace, votes over development. People's way of thinking has changed. Considering the burning issue of migration, the population of Mussoorie has blasted over the years and unfortunately, it continues to. The dreams and desires of an accomplished town fades into oblivion whenever we see Mussoorie facing the brunt of migration. We've addressed the pain that every lover of Mussoorie has been feeling but remains helpless. Through our helplessness emerges these poetries that throw light upon the condition of Mussoorie and its prospects. The poetic collection isn't a rebuke to the authorities but puts every resident under an examination. We can blame the authorities for not acting strictly but the onus also lies on its citizens. Not everything should need politics or an intervention of authorities. What sort of a future does Mussoorie actually hold. What all have this town of ours lost?

The collection doesn't have any connotations for politics but does specify politics of people responsible for the darkness of our present times. Things do emerge out of love like this very collection. And while we chose to delve into the realms of this darkness and bring out a light of hope, we too hope that the collection will inspire people to understand the gravity of the situation at this point of time and take a stand. We've seen the town evolving but to our shock, it has become a mere platform of experimentation. The collection has brought forth issues and touched upon stories of the town subtly. Every poem presents a unwavering longing mingling with an undying hope, calling upon the citizens to realize before it is late. The odes dedicated to the ancestors and River Ganga reiterate the urge to learn from the glorious past of Mussoorie and keep flowing like the River Ganga. Keeping alive the hope of preserving the legacy that we carry, it becomes significant to understand and realize the essence that the poems bring alive.

Through the poems, we have appealed to the residents of the town to wake up and preserve the fading emotions, heritage and glory of Mussoorie. The attempt is not to rewrite history but to awaken the 'lost generation' and make them realise their responsibility. The intention remains as pure as it can be— to offer something to our birthplace, our Queen of Hills, Mussoorie.

Introduction

Hundreds of men and women have lived here. So many generations have lived here. From the old Mussoorie to the present Mussoorie, I have been a witness to the changes. But in these changing times, there are so many things that make my town unique. The harmony with which people live and the culture of Mussoorie is remarkable. The love of people here, the care here makes Mussoorie like no other place. The feeling with which people talk...that feeling—only the people who have lived here and the people who are living here can understand. Yes, the Queen has been a symbol for life. From the peace and serenity of Sister's bazaar to the liveliness of Mall road and then to the peaceful life of Happy valley, Mussoorie has been gifted with rich heritage. There is an amalgamation of life and serenity. Whatever it is and whatever resources it had, people have lived here, the Queen has given shelter to uncountable people. I guess that's what places the town above everything. Every season makes the hearts feel blissful and this unites people. The cool winds touching the hearts, revive the tired souls. But then there are pangs too. There are longings of Landour, that is often considered as the old Mussoorie. There is an existential crisis which this part of my town faces. Ignorance and neglect is what it faces. It is longing for those days where nothing was politicised. There is a longing for a time when everyone felt like home in the town, where everyone felt a sense of connection, attachment and oneness. Longings hold the past memories. Longings are there for change but not at the cost of our heritage and culture. Longings that crave for an answer!

There are a lot of things that my town has seen. The journey has been full of turbulences. From my childhood till the present time, a lot of things have changed. A lot of people have sadly left us and a lot of people have migrated to different places especially to Dehradun. The entire town has changed. I agree that change is always for the better but there will always be a longing for the same town which I had seen in my childhood. There has come a major change but I have no choice than to accept everything— for all I can do is just long and be a voice for those who had some dreams for the town. A voice for those who want a town as peaceful as it was a decade or two ago. With technological advancements taking place, our authenticity and ethnicity must remain the same. We don't and we should definitely not forget the roots. In life whatever we become, our town and its people have an impact directly or indirectly.

Longings are for that landour where there is peace and happiness. Longings for the same greenery around. We'll always remain indebted to the ancestors of our town who have done a lot for its progress and unity. The spirit of Mussoorie and especially Landour lie in the hearts of all the people who have lived here and who are living here. Despite so many things coming our way, Landour has silently lived every moment and has seen itself and the country growing with time. Longings are for those days when original Landour was alive. A lot of work related to water and roads have taken place but in this world we need to let some things remain original- as they are. Longings of Landour are for the golden days of Landour, the golden period of Mussoorie. Longings are a hope for better days ahead and a better tomorrow inhibiting and holding back the past, the traditions, the culture of Landour that makes it rare and different from other places around. With the onset of each and every season, longings of Landour are a reflection on the days of Landour. The History of Mussoorie is very much incomplete without the history of Landour.

It's a longing to revive the lost glory of Landour. We have to revive Landour, the heart of Mussoorie. The way the people have lived their lives here reflect at the hope they carry for change and development while maintaining the original glory and authenticity. No one can ever find a place like Mussoorie that is blessed with the beauty of nature. No one can ever find a place like Mussoorie. No one can ever find a place like Landour. It is the legacy which we have to carry forward without changing its originality The glorious past cannot and should not be taken for granted or shouldn't be forgotten. The poems reflect on these dimensions.

❧ 1 ❧

There's nothing like hate,
In the story I'll narrate:
The tale of her birth,
And of becoming heaven on earth.
She's called the Queen,
Nature's beauty serene;
Not ignoring the tragic fate,
But still it isn't late
To leave our shallow pursuit
Of materialism and fame absolute!
The Queen calls,
Asking you and me to recall
The promise of selfless deeds,
And renouncing the greed.
The mirthful mourning,
And I see Landour longing!
Craving to elude the hypocrite minds,
And the selfish motives that hide.

Sigh?
No more a sigh!
The voice echoes,
To listen to the fading mellows.

2

An evening memorable,
Towards a fate inevitable;
Revisiting the lost time,
Finding words that would rhyme!
"Savage bull doth bear the yoke"
The glories it might revoke;
But the time has passed after all,
Amidst the promises tall,
Leaving the Queen with a hope, silently,
You should know the irony:
The Queen is still longing,
And her citizens mourning!
The night falls and reigns,
What has the Queen attained?
Solely, its history stained-
With the hues of materialists,
Who call themselves moralists.
The midnight hour is still away,
We shall wait for that bright day-
When someone would bring an end,
To the acts of those who pretend
To be the sole lovers of the town,
And proudly wear the jewelled crown.

Cry,
Or should I try?
When power is misused,
The glory is reduced.

❦ 3 ❦

I am the furious,
The one with a heart curious;
Perceptions offered,
Are now deferred!
They are ready to destroy,
And celebrate with joy:
The destruction of our heritage,
And there's no rage.
Call it unfortunate,
Or bitter fate:
They'll win through money,
And make it look ugly.
Now, they don't rule the heart,
But the minds and tear apart
The pages of our glorious history
Holding the traces of sustained liberty.
The rulers want to rule,
And call the citizens fool;
But forget that the voice once raised,
Will fade away the moments praised.
Reality is not tolerable,
And I'm not narrating a fable!

They lie,
Sigh!
The confrontation?
Or an introspection?

4

The woods in the landour
Are a wonder to explore;
But the plight
Makes me write:
The change that's happening,
It's challenging
To escape the embrace,
And the menace.
How should I sleep,
Seeing the Queen under the heap
Of cement clad construction-
In the dearth of a resolution
To leave behind the deadly dreams
And renouncing the cream;
For the sake of our Queen
Struck in a situation unforeseen.
The readers today,
I hope they may say
Loud and clear:
Their opinions without fear!
And step out of our narrow lanes,
And no effort shall go in vain.

The deodars are leaving,
Where is the fortune leaning?

❧ 5 ❧

On the roads,
Where politics is cut throat;
Where reality is highly different,
And men ignorant!
I wondered as a child,
On a wintry evening mild,
What should be his thoughts
As the town rots?
But there's nothing wrong
In being strong;
And speaking what the heart feels,
With a hope to heal!
It isn't a lamentation,
But a call for an introspection:
Lost love and gone glory,
Mocking at me for being gloomy?
Rest,
Who knows what is best?
The guide and the guardian?
A Historian?
Or a poet who has never been,
Or has seen
The future.

I'll tell you sincerely,
I'll speak fearlessly!

❦ 6 ❦

This isn't a cry,
But a life full of sighs;
This is a grief,
Giving us a moment brief
For instilling the empathy,
And realizing the lost legacy!
But ah! You're aware of this,
And will give it a miss.
The bells of the clock tower.

Empower

You and me to give reality, a voice,
Leaving us with no other choice!
To echo the truth down the lanes
Of landour ; Healing the pains,
Of our Queen, the giver,
And I expect you to differ!
The silence is no more alive,
For what should we strive?
Where has the town reached,
Abiding by what was preached!
No where, nothing!
Just wandering in the longings!
The heart on ground that rusts,
Had lived a life of hope and trusts!

~ **7** ~

The melody,
No more a remedy!
The Queen,
No more clean!
The loud cries,
Accompanied by teary eyes!

When tears dry,
And you wish to try;
Pick up a pen,
As you enter the glen-
And become a poet of nature,
Let love feature!
Detest the destructive development,
And honour the works eminent.
You read the words that were unwritten,
Unspoken and hidden;
And now, I speak what was the unheard,
There lies love in every word!
I am not the saviour,
But the one holding no fear
To ensure that 'love' is respected,
In deeds reflected.

Heal,
Fate: the future seals.

8

I don't call it a crisis,
For long, we haven't been decisive
With what the Queen needs!
And today, the poet bleeds:
To lament at the loss,
And focus on the pros and cons;
We together are responsible,
But none is accountable!
Call it a sad plight,
Or desire's might!
The trees of the landour,
And the rain that pour,
No more give me that transcendental innocence,
And I am left but to show indifference!
The long lost love is now a story,
Relating to the undying spirit of Mussoorie's glory!
We'll fight with ourselves,
But what about the greed that dwells
In the so called lovers-
Wishing that the Queen recovers.
And she's been waiting,
And I've been writing!

The roads are silent,
Resilient!

❧ 9 ❧

I wander through the woods,
And do what a poet should-
Reach Sir Everest's abandoned abode,
And there's end to the road!
Once, the Hermit's home,
Today, no one roams:
You and I are going there,
To see what the future bears-
Looking at the Queen's struggles,
I wait for her revival!
Sir Everest's dreams are long forgotten,
And we are the fallen
Leaves of the autumns,
With hymns solemn-
The dancing pollens of the springs,
And the rains which the monsoon brings!
The seasonal politicians are in demand,
Here, honesty will not stand!
Poets will come and die,
And here, only the love will sigh!
Hold on,
The good days haven't yet gone.

Feel free, dear heart,
For a hope, this is a start!

10

Humans, they say,
Had had their good day!
At the cost of nature,
Which now lies in danger!
But I hear the murmurs,
They are celebrating with fervour
The gentle arrival of desire,
And tell me to admire
The Queen who is lamenting-
But there's a meaning-
In every act that hurts
And the hatred that takes birth!
I'll hold on and write,
About the glories and sight
The assumptions that dwell in the mind,
That no where else, I can find!
The moonlight is no more pure,
I've lost my cure-
To my anxious being,
And all my screaming!
The silence has gone away,
For which I am longing every day.

Silence spiritual,
The nature performs a ritual!

❧ 11 ❧

Towards a more silent spot,
With hundreds of thoughts
Striking this chaotic mind,
And nothing I find!
Why?
Will my passion die?
The reason of this chaos,
But the thought of being yours-
Dear Queen, is so soothing,
But there's something
Which isn't the same!
Destroyed only to be called by a name:
Mussoorie and her glories
Her people and their pleasant stories
Have gone away far,
May be watching us like the stars
Watch us every night,
And make us write
Tales of lamentation and happiness,
All belonging to the wilderness!
Where are you?
The silence under the sky blue?

Time will still,
If the Queen will.

12

Under an oak tree,
I'll find thee—
Dear Queen, still living!
Shattered yet forgiving
Your most loved children.
There's nothing hidden
In between the trees
And the roads that never cease
To amuse the passionate
Heart that longs to advocate-
The laws of nature supreme,
And that visionary gleam!
All have gone, disappeared,
The glory is still revered-
Devotion through the darkness,
We are turning heartless!
Why do I still hope this sincerely?
Why do I still look forward desperately?
Maybe, the Queen is asking me,
To see
And not lose hope in humanity,
There's more to the sincerity!

I'll wait,
And advocate!

❧ 13 ❧

Don't seek refuge in denial,
Focus on the revival;
The brutality visible,
My Queen seems miserable.
So many questions,
No time for reflection—
But why should they?
All they can do is play
With the legacy we all own,
Attacking the Queen's throne.
I seek neither praise nor fame,
Or participate in the game;
But I wish to reach out,
Inform and not shout.
Sometimes, it feels tough,
Looking at the behavior rough
But the love transcends everything,
And light of hope it brings:
Every line calling for introspection,
Despite the desperation!
Every word opening eyes,
Despite the sighs!

❧ **14** ❧

Pray!
As they say;
When there's nothing you can do,
Not a single clue!
But actions should be done,
And elections won!
There are accounts of men nameless,
Confessing of their acts shameless.
Should I raise voice,
I'll have no other choice
Than to face the dying dreams,
And scream, yes, scream!
How do I pray,
And break the cliché?
Don't fear-
I'll make them hear
Again and again,
That love will not go in vain!
My Queen will rise,
And bring out all the lies!
You and I will witness,
The words of the Fearless.

Remember,
The lover!

❧ **15** ❧

You and I, with intentions pure,
Are resolved to cure
The dry weather of the town
And restore the faded crown!
But they shall laugh and mock,
Aloud, they'll talk-
And do nothing for her sake-
Giving you and me, a heart ache.
I'll find some one speaking reality,
Transcending this mortality:
Leaving impressions indelible,
With arguments credible.
The deodar trees are dying,
Future eyeing
At a time when life would be tough,
And nature rough-
In Her approach to mankind,
Renouncing the virtue of being kind!
You and I
Will sigh!
What else should we expect
From the sincerity left!

Who am I to comment?
It is a warning that I had sent!

❧ 16 ❧

Embrace,
The fallen race
With a grave face-
And undying pace!
The Queen and my love exists,
But my soul resists
To accept this harsh truth,
And reject the behaviour uncouth.
All seems to be a dream,
Of milk with cream;
Of springs with fallen leaves,
Of an illusion that deceives.
The voice will disappear,
And you'll no longer hear:
The touching cry of the lover,
Forced to rediscover
The melody of the nightingale,
Which now tells the tale
Of the town- to the woods,
Revisiting the inevitable moods!
But the lost has gone forever,
There's pain in every tear!

I'll wait patiently,
I'll accept graciously.

17

Today,
Humbly, I'll say;
Every street has a dream in politics,
And the greed that sticks-
Sucks every drop of blood,
And every hope dies in this flood-
Waiting for you and me,
To feel, cry and agree-
With the oblivion that confronts,
And interrupts
Our peaceful approach to life here,
There's a limit to which the Queen can bear.
There's nothing wrong with intentions,
I call for introspection!
When love shall overpower,
YOU and I will empower
The Queen and advocate-
Our purpose great;
Devoted to the Queen and her sister,
The Nature— fond of showing the mirror
To the mankind,
And peace- we'll find!

Truth transcends humanity,
Calling out for sincerity!

18

It's the longing,
Of My Queen's belongings-
The heritage age old,
Was shamelessly sold!
The nature, on death bed-
You and I still respected;
But you see the power of love, dear
With every drop of my tear-
Revived:
Survived!
My Queen!
Green.
I lost myself, that day,
Or a sacrifice: you may say-
I am living to heal,
With the evils, I deal-
For I am left spellbound,
When nature surrounds;
And I've nothing else,
But to feel the pulse
Of the Queen now,
You and I have taken a vow!

Who knows what's fit?
When you are being killed bit by bit!

≈ 19 ≈

Something fills the air,
Invoking those who care-
The Laburnum blooms,
Its scent looms
The presiding deity,
With the sense of royalty!
I adore the wonderous
Ways of nature and the generous
Queen that still awaits,
A lover who states-
Strong facts over greedy emotions,
And acts with devotion!
The sly and the jealous,
The evil and the rebellious-
Hold nothing but hatred,
You and I will get betrayed!
Feel free,
To climb the oak tree:
Watching the nature as it passes,
Notice: the time pauses!
Glad, we met,
Others have already slept!

Lover, are you fake?
Or a change, you are eager to make?

20

Sleep well,
I hear some people tell
The tales of the lost heritage-
They were in rage!
I hear them,
From the realms-
Of their emotions,
Destroying the notions
Of showing up as strong-
But there's nothing wrong
In revisiting the lost chambers,
When the Queen was pampered!
They mention of 'The Rink',
You and I are forced to think-
What was it?
Where does the wind sit?
They skated and skated,
With these thoughts, I am elated!
You and I can still skate
For name sake and wait:
Change- it is called,
Our Queen is enthralled!

They'll burn every such dream down,
And wonder what happened to the town!

21

Silence is special,
It has that potential-
To change and to murder
The Hopes not willing to surrender!
I'm bewildered and shocked,
I'm the voice that is mocked:
But one day,
You may find a way—
To read these pages of our past,
And things will surely contrast;
It's not the time to cry,
Or asking me why!
The change is certain,
And I'll see with the lantern-
The traces,
Goddess Fortune embraces!
Hold on,
Lead on!
I can hear the stories,
Never found in between the diaries!
Blessed and the happiest,
Living with moments sweetest!

Love, where were you then?
Help them again!

22

"You ignore that pain,
And call me insane!
Laugh at me,
When no hopes I see:
Destroy my roots,
Stay indifferent to what nature attributes !
I am the Queen,
An evidence to the men mean!
How do I bear?
With whom should I share?
Who cares?
Will someone dare
To raise the voice!
Which isn't their choice-
Killing me won't save them,
Who is responsible for the mayhem?"
I replied,
"Hopes have died-
Lovers have gone away,
We're surely having a dull day!
But at who's behest,
These parasites rest!"

I don't have an answer,
You are my anchor!

❦ 23 ❦

I'll walk down to the lake,
And peace I make-
With the chaos that's present,
I'll repent!
The charm
Did no harm
To you and me, did it?
Then why do they hit-
Again and again desperately,
Their acts harm subtly-
The Queen's silence,
Helped their violence
Grow-
And the seeds of destruction they sow,
In loneliness,
I find the bliss of loveliness-
And the longing lies ignored,
In response, not a word
From the so called seasonal lovers-
Who wait for things to recover:
And then arrive-
They talk and revive,
The Queen.

Sigh!

24

The mechanical age,
Causes rage!
But they think, it's fine,
Not to dine
With memories,
Then they eat with ease:
The glory, the love and the greenery,
To wait for their end eagerly!
To the cloud end,
Where men pretend-
To be the admirers
And the explorers
Of the town which once held
Pride, is now compelled-
To sleep-
For the darkness is deep!
The Queen is silent,
On an evening vibrant;
Silence is power, they say,
There's no other way!
Broken by the noise of the cars,
They are craving for an applause.

You and I,
Watching all this with teary eyes.

25

The tale isn't humiliating,
Our acts are devastating!
Say goodbye to the trees,
In a way that no one sees!
The humble nature now revolts,
You and I still behold
The beauty that lies in the realms
Of the Queen who rebels!
She's not at fault,
No one ever thought:
How beauty could become a curse,
And I'll be writing melancholic verse-
To revisit, revive and re-establish
The glory, ready to vanish!
'Emotions are dead',
Somewhere I had read.
But when it comes to survival,
There's no denial!
Queen has been generous,
We have turned treacherous-
In our thoughts and in deeds,
Ignoring what the queen needs!

We'll be free-
Together, the world will see.

26

Pardon me,
Have a look at my plea-
When the mind resists,
To accept the situation that persists:
And there's no one willing-
To see the Queen healing;
To revive the old time,
When the crown used to shine!
But somewhere I feel,
It is difficult to deal
With the change that is happening,
Eluding is challenging!
Don't misunderstand me,
You're free to disagree!
I'm not wrong-
In showing that we are strong
Enough to make things beautiful,
And being careful
In revisiting the stories forgotten,
In the season of autumn!
Those who helped the Queen flourish,
Golden moments, let them cherish.

Roar,
You'll see the nature soar!

27

You and I won't judge,
But every numb heart, we'll touch-
And the pain will be cured,
I am assured!
I'll be hated and loved,
I know I'll be judged!
But the sense of attachment
And a craving for spiritual advancement-
Takes me forward,
As the hatred is cornered;
And love for my Queen Reigns,
But the moment that remains
Calls for you and me, sincerely,
Not to feel sad bitterly,
But to voice out!
With no doubt.
And yes, dear reader,
You are our future leader-
Let no rage discourage you,
Let no rival undermine you!
Do not forget,
The bright night after the sunset!

At the camel's back,
The silence comes back!

❧ **28** ❧

Where's it gone?
Why do I mourn?
The rendition of our times,
No more seems to rhyme!
Love fades,
As migration invades-
And the heart turns emotionless,
At the state of hopelessness!
But you and I still sing that song-
Which nature enthuses along!
The Queen isn't angry,
But sad at the fancy:
The acts unacceptable,
The tears unbearable-
Of the lovers who still talk
And ignore those who mock!
Remember the trees green,
That gave beauty to the Queen;
And peace to my mind,
When no hope I could find!
Good sense still prevails,
Even when silence fails.

In the bazaars of landour,
Love, we'll crave for!

29

A collapse?
Or an increasing gap
Between reality and illusion,
Between chaos and seclusion!
My town isn't the same,
Lacking its natural frame;
They'll not hesitate
To dictate
The means to recover-
And ways they'll discover
To revive the Queen now!
They'll utter anyhow!
The whispers are pain bearing,
There's no one hearing!
They'll define,
They'll design!
And ask us our responsibility,
Ignoring their sincerity-
In stating facts and not greed,
Invoking when there's a need!
Just like the leaf with morning dew,
I write for lovers few!

O Queen,
No one will contravene!

🌿 **30** 🌿

Miles to walk,
A lot to talk:
About the fight,
I wish to write-
A fight for a state,
Fought by our fighters great;
The cable cars go up and down,
Witnessing the life in the town!
Still,
Noise- ready to kill!;
Loved,
Succumbed.
And life goes on,
Silence from the dusk to the dawn!
The rainy days are still waiting
To come and help us in breathing;
The forest fires are now choking,
Some days are provoking-
To find the Queen amidst the smoke-
Like the canvas with black strokes.
Alas, what has happened!
Saddened.

No, not hopeless,
You and I are homeless!

31

The incensed breeze
Blows with the intention to tease;
Sitting beneath the deodar tree,
Its the change I see!
The longing
Of this summer morning-
Is strong and sublime-
Leaving impressions on the sands of time!
This midnight grief,
Isn't brief,
It holds the pain of ages,
The power trapped in cages!
Of dreams that are now dead,
Of greed to slyly earn the bread.
Unprecedented,
The Queen lamented
At the fate-
She had nothing to state!
Let the voice reach seven skies,
To evoke the man who tries
To sympathize,
And for revival- emphasize!

Dark and deep,
Everyone is fast asleep!

32

Longing rare,
No one ready to care-
Finding reasons,
And politics of different seasons!
There is nothing left,
To detest;
But the silence of a few,
Amidst the darker hue
Is painful and sinful-
And the Queen is tearful.
Come along,
From the dusk until the dawn;
Let's go for a walk and sing that song,
Till the highest point of the town!
The Rhododendron's sweetness,
Filling the air with tenderness-
The wind's gentleness,
Bearing the nectar of divine consciousness.
When nature surrounds,
And no one is around;
Nothing is left for us to strive-
It feels as if the Heaven has come alive!

Let the wind blow,
With it, our love flows.

❧ 33 ❧

On a snowy day,
When the sun is away-
Some guests do arrive,
Somehow live and survive!
Who knows what the Queen offers,
The great nation honours-
This gift of nature,
Which now is in danger.
Existential crisis, dear!
But they won't fear.
What if the Queen narrates,
Every fact it states!
Will the flatterers utter,
And show their true colour;
When these guest show their back,
Tell me, what do we lack?
No accountability!
Is it inevitability?
The wintry breeze,
Begins to cease-
And I'm lost in the desert,
As destruction takes its birth.

Nothing else to say,
We were having a good day.

❧ 34 ❧

The tales of innocence,
Bearing the course of coincidence;
From British legacy,
To the hills of ecstasy!
The church bell rings,
And the wind embracing the violin strings;
In every thing, there are traces,
As time embraces.
Feel free, here,
Hear:
The Himalayan birds,
As I long for a word-
A word from sincere silence-
Through the years of violence;
Every act to kill the soul
Of the Queen; now in control!
Look for the impressions that are fading,
As the human footprints are invading;
Recover,
It is the longing of the lover:
Feel it deeply,
Accept the reality, completely.

Come soon,
Before it's noon.

❈ 35 ❈

The waves of change strike,
A change- no one would like!
You and I will manage-
When we reach our old age,
To relate to the golden era,
And the wind bearing plethora
Of emotions intense,
Creating a suspense.
And some where, we'll relive,
To insist and forgive-
Those who gave us our present,
And the generations that would repent!
Don't forget the days when we struggled,
When the ruler was humbled
By the voice of God,
And men were eager to applaud.
Read the hills of hope and history,
Bring an end to this mystery-
Whose fault was it?
Why was the Queen hit
By the demons of greed?
What was the need?

Long live our past,
Let our love forever last.

❧ **36** ❧

A sense of discomfort,
Pride ending as a mirth!
Longing is strong,
But to whom does the fault belong?
I'll sing a song, nevertheless,
To lament the acts of men careless;
If not hatred, what else should we call-
The rise of the Queen and her Fall!
The embodiment of pride,
Yes, the gift which nature provides-
And there's no one to define,
Supposedly mine but never became mine!
The testimony we bear,
And the tales, we can no more hear!
The bold voices are in grave-
Remembered for their acts to save-
The Queen and the future unknown,
Today, we only mourn.
The tower is brought down,
There's no rage in the town.

Month of springs arrive,
Allowing you and me to survive.

❧ **37** ❧

Read aloud,
As the monsoon clouds
Break the awkward silence of the season,
Who knows what's the reason?
The heavy flow of water on ground,
And only rainwater surrounds-
The idea of sublime
And it might take time
For us to adapt,
And understand the fact:
Change has been deadly,
Shame on those who create a medley
Of our sorrow and pain,
But what can one gain,
From resolving to change,
And making things look strange!
They say it is a phase,
But the lovers never did chase
The dreams of modern hollow,
And their aspirations are shallow!

Great glorious graceful time,
All lost in the sands of time.

❧ 38 ❧

Call this a love story,
Bearing pages, full of irony-
Not a conventional
Love- don't be skeptical
Of the Queen and her lover,
Gracing the love that would empower;
And recreate the lost connection,
Ensuring my salvation!
Don't think, I am sad,
But if words I had-
To question the greed and the greedy,
And those who pretend to be cheeky.
This tale would be eternal,
Transcending the being mortal!
You are a lover, today,
She's the Queen, who may
Lose her voice tomorrow,
And the moments of sorrow-
Would enter like the dark night
That ends a day bright!

Legacy,
Craving for empathy.

39

I think, I should rest,
I can't see the hill's crest-
Dearth of beauty,
And of our glory, truly.
You and I are listening,
Eyes, like the stars twinkling-
With the hope of revival,
No moments are, for us, final
To feel like it's the end,
For rising has always been in trend!
And the fire that burns within,
May somehow destroy their sin.
The history borne by an elite trees,
And their account resists to cease:
For they were there, before me,
After me, they'll be the ones to see-
May be,
Let's see!
Wait for an awakening?
But the destiny is threatening.

Stay calm?
Sing a psalm.

40

Being a witness to the lost time,
I'll accept graciously, the fault of mine
In believing in the promises of today,
Which otherwise had no say!
The witnesses-
At the verge of craving and sadness;
Know they'll cry any time,
Who knows whether they'll accept this time?
They promised of something better,
But gave us a reality bitter-
Of hatred and of curse,
And these things are not worse-
The Queen has lost a lot before
I could write an elegy and explore
The reason and find the murderers,
But they won't surrender.
Still,
Your heart, you can fill-
With the ashes of peace and bliss,
And the Queen you can miss.

She's gone, forever,
I'll find her last letter!

❧ 41 ❧

A silent healing,
After a lot of screaming;
Of noise we'll never talk about,
And breed a generation of doubt.
Hollow foundation to the structure,
That might save the culture-
But the legacy is not yet lost,
Don't ask me what is the cost-
Of losing the age old tower
And bathroom tiles they'll shower-
On it and there it wishes,
As the glory diminishes.
Many are angry,
But I'll tell you frankly,
The dying dreams are full of longings,
Craving for a belonging,
The long ques to visit the ill queen,
And they are keen-
To help her stay prosperous,
But their ignorance is dangerous.
And we are ignorant,
Not innocent.

Do you listen,
The guilty won't be forgiven.

❧ 42 ❧

Look at the valley,
People aren't at all happy!
Long ques at the entry gates,
Waiting- Who doesn't hate!
But that's the fate, I believe
And the rulers deceive-
It's fine and obvious
To remain unconscious
For the citizens up here,
Don't fear,
But remain calm and compliant,
Resolved to remain quiet.
Hold on there,
Pride dares
To cheat and defeat
The dying legacy; our ancestors greet-
And we remain grateful,
And of course careful-
In relating to the times that have been glorious,
Who knows who'll be victorious.
Heal,
Feel.

Rise,
With sighs.

❧ 43 ❧

The crowded streets are a boon,
Things will change soon-
And the town will be a city,
A matter of universal pity!
I know lost time won't be back,
There are things you and I lack-
Not maturity to accept
The harsh present of men who have nothing to regret.
But the sense of acceptance,
That struggles through the corridors of resistance;
This tale is a composition,
Telling you and me, our position:
The ideological battle eager to touch the ground,
And affect each one around,
But who knows things will change for a better,
I can't find the Queen's last letter.
The letter full of agony,
The words bearing the entire galaxy;
Each line holding a truth transcendental,
Asking us to be gentle.
Heal,
Feel.

The universe torn apart,
Even before the start.

44

I found some torn pages,
Holding pain of many ages-
On the lanes of Landour lying,
As the soul of the Queen is dying.
Just one last word,
Unheard;
With every bit of the pages torn,
A new story was born-
The melancholic verses,
Seemed to me, curses:
And eager to find,
I lost my mind
In between the woods,
Witnessing my various moods!
You lost it,
I lost it.
But the hope lives on,
Even after the Queen has gone.
They'll erect a replica of the Queen,
And keep it clean!
My Queen will be forgotten,
Like the leaves that fall in autumn.

Cry,
Sigh.

45

It's yet again cloudy,
Most of us, here moody-
Getting ready for a walk,
And no one can talk!
Let thoughts flow,
Giving hypocrisy a blow-
Don't mind my words,
They are not worth
Your time; They are powerful
For those who are beautiful-
In their thoughts and efforts,
And somewhere give me comfort
Temporary,
Like in a life solitary!
The peace still exists,
In the places that resist-
To accept the humiliation of man,
Yes, nature can!
The roads to Lal tibba will!
The silence stands still.

Dear,
The future isn't clear!

46

The gun hill,
They're ready to kill!
The cannon lies there,
In no one's care!
Abandoned,
I'm saddened;
But not a word uttered,
Not a person buttered!
No voice raised,
And commercial life chased
The dying legacy too-
With an intention to woo!
But then there's this love, I believe,
Which can never deceive!
And the passion that burns,
Are but thorns-
Which now make this poet bleed
Words that rebuke the greedy and the greed!
Selfless spirits,
Recreating the moments vivid-
Of the gone days and the longing,
Craving for a belonging.

Not a tear,
But fear.

❧ 47 ❧

A pause,
Without a cause-
An escape-
And future, we'll shape!
Through the darkness of greed,
Let us sow the seeds-
Of selflessness and loyalty,
Bring an end to our innate cruelty!
Way ahead,
And there are emotions dead
In this world of love and happiness,
Now lies under the cover of sadness!
But some how,
You'll bow!
At the magic that the Queen bestow,
A different world, it bounds to show!
A peace, still alive,
For harmony, people here will strive!
Not broken by hearts,
But the legacy that we no longer support.

Hail!
Fail.

48

Not an end to this story,
That remembers the Queen's glory-
I'm lost in the thoughts,
And suddenly see a clot-
An increase in the cars,
Are but scars-
A means to livelihood,
For a shelter and some food!
But they'll ignore,
Allow some greed to soar;
For the bazar of Landour,
They've found no cure:
Forgotten,
Rotten!
In pain, I write,
When no hope is in sight!
Longing fails to find solace,
And hopes chase:
The dying legacy of the legend,
Some where, I'm reckoned.

Wait,
Don't hate.

49

My Queen, then and now,
I'll utter if my tears allow-
The solace I found then,
And I didn't pick my pen
To write the glorious years,
Forgotten amidst the drops of tears;
The route to the Happy valley,
Choked by the machines, sadly.
And no houses are locked here,
For people are entering without fear-
For a life and a living,
And the crisis is deepening!
My Queen is bearing,
My Queen is hearing;
My Queen is longing,
Landour is longing.
Revisit,
A bit.
And a life is lived, once again,
Efforts don't go in vain.
Oh! A new year wish,
Can we change all this?

Understand.

50

The lodges up the hill,
Are calling you and me to be still
And once again re-live the gone days,
The bliss stays!
Chaos and noise now dominates,
The silence waits-
Crimson hues of the dying sun,
Leaving a trail of memories and of fun.
Don't be obliged,
Let love preside
Your mind and your heart
And let us together start:
A reverse migration-
A movement blessed with an affirmation:
To bring alive the time peaceful,
When the knowledgeable were careful
And delicately protected the integrity-
With love of greatest intensity.
We are all fake,
Advantage we take-
Of the silence of our Queen,
For her well being- none of us are keen.

Sigh.
Lest we try.

❧ 51 ❧

The silence near the cemetery,
Is not scary-
For it is the mourning of the loss,
And the concern of the cosmos.
The longing of the past,
Peace would no longer last;
The silence amidst the graves,
Of the English and the locals brave-
Uttering 'Amen'
To avoid the Mayhem;
The prayers are endless,
And love limitless.
Their letters haven't reached yet,
The sun has set!
Their love still felt,
Feel and your heart will melt-
The flowers that lie on the graves solemnly
Fill with their fragrance, the air of the country-
So sweet,
A treat
For our soul-
Leading us to the inevitable goal.

Visit,
Do not resist.

52

The serenity of Jabarkhet,
And heaven, the nature creates;
For those who have loved sincerely,
And handled dearly-
The crown of the Queen,
Snatched from the mean
And the longing has to wait,
To be satisfied and meditate:
Over the loss and the restoration,
Over the destruction and creation!
And renewal of hope-

Seclusion,
Antithetical to delusion:
And the craving continues,
As we choose,
Life and not an absolute end,
Things might mend,
And the fog embraces-
As we lose our traces-
Uncertain, unfortunate,
It is still not late!

Left and right,
No one is sight.

53

The wind blows,
Monsoon rains slow:
And green and green,
Special and serene!
The seasonal lovers arrive,
Who hate to revive
What has gone into the oblivion,
And utter a few idioms
Which might heal
The scars and deal
With the longing and the loneliness,
Dearth of holiness!
And a few letters that I receive-
Love, I perceive!
Every place has a story,
Every person sorry!
And then a few: not ready to worry-
A burden they carry!
The Himalayan club days,
And the alternate ways-
The curls of the Queen,
Are but the roads unseen

And uncared-
Some not yet discovered.

54

Deceit and dissent,
Political advantage it may lent-
And that's a curse with a cure,
But I'm not sure
If we poets can change,
And make things look no longer strange—
For people like you and me
Secluded from the so called free,
Who fight and preserve
The integrity, my Queen deserves;
You see these petty minds,
Performing drama of many kinds!
They'll dance on the political rendition,
And question me for this new tradition!
Could I expect more?
From those who only wish to conquer!
But no one could ever escape
When it was about landour landscape!
And the longing, my dear
With respect, I adhere
The destiny that makes me wait,
And it isn't late!

Hush!
Don't rush!

❧ 55 ❧

How should I speak?
With my heart this weak!
And as I witness
The cause of the darkness-
My words hold silence,
Maybe a defiance:
Let the change come,
And a lot of things done!
A better illusion for a bitter reality,
Providing food for the insanity!
These words aren't blunt,
I wish to confront-
The shallowness that dares,
Ignorant of what is fair!
You and me are helpless,
They'll destroy the tenderness
That dwells in the longings,
Causing in the modern lodgings.
We as writers will question,
And revive the lost impression
Of a cleaner, greener town-
A diamonds in the crown.

A word or a two for those,
Who are thorns in this rose!

❦ **56** ❦

Divisions and decisions,
Leading to frictions:
And I see the inevitable coming,
Amidst the birds humming!
In search of a reason to walk
Up the hill from Jharipani and talk
About the course of time,
When the wind hunts for signs
Of changes as they plan a revenge-
Oh! I've reached Barlowganj!
Yes, silence is felt
This heart melts
But I miss the falls,
As if something calls
Me back to the lost time,
Restoring the glorious paradigm—
In search of peace, I wander-
There's solace yonder!
Reason and sensibilities,
Passion and possibilities-
Struggle to live and grow
As the pseudo rise their eyebrow!

"It is fine", I am told
To keep some stories untold!

❧ **57** ❧

To keep them untold,
And losing the hold
Of our stories and the longing,
No sense of a belonging-
Fate and the fallen all lie,
Emotions are high:
Let me stick to the mankind,
As the money grinds
This crown of Queen now purloined,
And a new term is coined-
Lovers of the Queen!
Ah! Not mean;

Know the plot,
As the Queen rots-
I'm hoping to tell,
Elude as this turns a hell;
But the dawn is near,
I'm filled with fear-
As love craves to create
A difference, the world would hate.

Or forget if there's a tomorrow
With a paucity of sorrow!

❧ **58** ❧

Furious and full of fire,
Lies an unprecedented desire
To restore what remains lost and gone,
And Pages written and torn!
Tell me not who did what—
Tell me, who really fought
For the sake of my Queen,
Who vowed to protect the hills green!
Undermined and ignored are these urges,
But as the voices merge,
I'm hopeful of that realization
An eye opener for an utter temptation;
This soliloquy will remain unheard,
All statements of truth would be called a mirth—
But look, I'm here to write,
Day and night,
With ink indelible,
And words that are reliable!
For someday in future,
These words would nurture
Minds that would think,
And eyes that would blink!

Ink stains aren't called a blot,
But speak a lot!

59

Before fades my ink,
I should write about the skating rink—
A heritage burnt and lost forever,
A loss we could never recover;
Standard Grand Skating Rink was the name,
Blessed by fortune and immense fame:
Call it a cradle of memories,
And of infinite stories-
Now a thing of our past,
"If only it could last"
—I hear the witnesses wishing,
I too join them in hoping,
But what is in our hands?
Where do we stand?
The skates no longer roll,
An unprecedented unfortunate hault!
Queen wonders in pain,
What was her gain?
We fail to realize,
I'm left with sighs
For the gold that we've lost—
Oh Queen!

Seeing the past of glories,
Future and present hold worries!

60

My eyes are moist,
For the glory we've lost!
The one's who left us midst the journey—
And I am seeking solace in the stories,
So many unanswered questions live on,
The moments, the mellows are forever gone:
And through these words with haste of mortality —
I long to give my Queen a taste of eternity;
Look for that immortal trace,
Blessed and gifted by divine grace-
Live the moments that would never return,
And no more mourn!
Preserve what exists with us now,
Seek refuge in the heritage anyhow.
I have but tears to offer,
To my muse— the Divine power
For guiding me page by page,
Revisiting the roads of bygone age:
Regardless of the sunsets I've missed,
I've truly been blessed!
Words have spoken reality,
With love and sincerity!

With a strong sense of belonging,
There continues the longings!

**Solemn words carry deep emotions,
some feelings carry deep meanings.**

61

An ode to my town,
Faith won't let us down.
Over the mountains,
And above the valley.
Exists my town strong,
Strong beyond the wrong.
With clouds hovering,
I feel the world through it.
Seeing the lives—
Much more beautiful,
Much peaceful.
I know it has been long,
But there strikes a realization
Of passion for my town.
Where talent is endless,
And no one becomes hopeless.
I'll write for my town,
Till my last breath.
For it won't let me down,
And keep me away from love's death!

62

Amidst the clouds,
There shines my town.
Where change is permanent,
And its soil— vehement.
I come from a town,
Where love held its roots.
Where humanity prevailed,
But today, I see things missing there.
A lost connection with everyone there,
I know a place like this is rare.
And trail of the bygone days,
Reminds me of the silence that once prevailed.
I won't talk of change,
For nothing definitely remains the same.
This is a place where nature beholds,
And every day, a new story unfolds.
People with good hearts here,
But have we remained the same here?
A place where truth unfolds,
History repeating at every fold!

✿ **63** ✿

The residents were blessed—
I saw them hoping
For peace and serenity.
The Town served people,
For ages they've seen the steep hills.
Never complained,
Never left.
I lived and loved,
Those mountains were loved.
I have seen the beginning,
I've seen the end.
I've seen my town growing,
Within and within, I have seen it dying.
To whom should I say,
With whom should I share?
I'll write to heal,
To glorify again, I'll plead.

❧ 64 ❧

To the town that I love,
I knew how blessed I was!
I saw the silence speak.
I saw the ruins swell;
Still I craved to tell the world,
That this beauty was rare.
And then there were some far away from it,
Never valued the glory of the town.
Having been born here was a blessing,
Through difficulties and yet smiling—
Together we grew,
The oneness of the hearts divine.
And still something lacked,
A town once full packed
Or the silence, we all wanted,
A confusion in my mind,
The heart restless tonight.

65

With love,
For my town, I write.
Where silence is disturbed today,
And the higher ups have a key role to play.
"Let those elite have a say"
And make the rest, victims of their game.
I am seeing a future gloomy,
If this continues, it will benefit some.
Under the umbrella, I saw things going,
Where true sense of my town, I saw missing.
Maybe personal interests haunts today,
But is there any other way?
Things going almost the same,
Decades and decades, I feel no change.
They come and they go,
Every time, they make me feel low.
Restless is my town,
Finding hope even as the sun sets down!

— 66 —

The Town knows the pain,
But still no one cares.
Problems and Problems,
Without seeking a solution.
A Town grows with people,
I remember, they say!
We live here for long,
Singing the glorious songs.
Songs bringing the past alive,
Keeping the future alive, Sigh!
I hear the song of birds now,
Maybe they have been here for long now.
From evolution to realization,
The Town has guided my passion.
The Town holds history,
Hiding several mysteries.
Every bend has a story,
And you— don't worry.
I'll tell the story,
For every mountain carries beauty!

❧ **67** ❧

To my town in my heart,
Hope your silence lasts.
Your beauty lies in simplicity,
Emerging out from humility!
Though change is certain,
But how could I see the Queen in pain!
They say, they are changing for good,
But how can my heart accept the truth.
The higher ups responsible,
For ruining my town now.
Everything lost in politics,
What else we have now.
They suppress the voice
Of my town and my fellows.
Silence is justified,
But what shall 'Silence' do now.
Who helps in Nature's restoration,
Who really has true aspirations?

❧ **68** ❧

A confused heart wandering,
For reality, my heart is wondering.
Is it the greed for means,
That is ruining my town?
The Queen bearing all the pains,
In greed, no one actually gains.
For a long time, I didn't write,
Just wanted to let the Queen heal on its own.
But greed increased,
Nature's destruction rose.
No one cared for greeneries around,
Very less greenery now surrounds!
Nature— beauty of my town,
That never wishes to bring me down.
A true friend and a companion, indeed,
All lost in the greed.
The queen pleads,
Hope there were people to heal!

❧ 69 ❧

Admire the beauty of my town,
Where clouds make you feel sound.
Where mornings are energetic,
And evenings are peaceful.
Where sun rises with hope,
And the sun sets— calming us all down.
I belong to a town,
Where nature holds the way.
You are always in the lap,
Never beyond or away.
But I see, something different now,
I don't feel the same now.
The ways seems to have changed,
A new life being traced—
I belong to a town,
For which I feel proud.
But the change is bad,
It does make us sad.

❦ 70 ❦

I have seen the change,
And how beautiful things are no more the same.
A place that once was decorated by greeneries,
Lies devastated today!
Nature's love changed
Or Mussoorie is left to be blamed.
I hear and hold,
As in words, the pain unfolds.
I know its late,
But we just can't accept the fate
To save the identity
Of our Queen!
To make everyone realize,
Before it is too late.
I have seen the vigour in hearts,
To do something for the town,
But how should one ?
When no one cares about you.

We need to realize,
And not empathize.

71

A place
Where nature rules,
Where life is at slow pace,
But do we really care?
I come from a place,
Where clouds embrace,
And hearts get filled with joy—
But who values it?
I expected everyone
But no one admired the nature.
Not everyone can see that beauty,
Not everyone can feel the bliss!
I have lived that way,
Allowing nature to heal the hearts;
From the chaos of the world,
Letting her bring peace to my heart.
I wait for that heavenly boon,
May the realization come soon!

72

I know it hurts,
To see the greenery get lost.
I know it makes us think
Of the people living here,
The changes in sight!
The ruins turning into plights.
I have seen the town
Diving deep into politics.
The trees will tell you,
How much they have suffered.
Or speak to the age-old houses,
Where they are standing alone.
It hurts to see all this—
A civilization not meant to change.
Greatness in difference, is rare,
To the history, let's not stare.
For a flourishing future awaits—
Understand, before it's too late.

73

Often, a place needs change,
To ensure things don't become strange!
But today, we don't feel the same,
The town has changed.
I notice an imprint of the ancestors,
Longing for their compassionate shelter.
The land cries for justice,
As the heart turns numb.
My town seeks that Golden time,
Has anyone heard the Queen's cry?
And those omnipresent trees,
Have seen it all—
The rise and fall of the town,
Seen the ones who brought took away the crown!
Nothing around,
The Nature here makes one sound.
The change is here,
Even the fruits that it bear!

74

I never expected
The Queen to be misdirected—
The loss she couldn't afford,
And the beauty was ignored!
The 'lovers' chose money
Finding their way to harmony;
The 'lovers' wanted change,
But it is useless to rage.
Speak but speak low—
My Queen suffers, I know.
And so the beauty is vanishing
Cars up and down rushing.
Buildings rising everywhere,
To breathe, there's no fresh air.
I know, I'm late,
Should we depend completely on fate!
I remember, my town bright,
Resisting to see this plight!
To feel for the Queen
Isn't a crime,
But to see the people losing their way,
Only to harm their town!
Every corner still sings,
And divine joy it brings—
All you need to do is hear,
But there's no one here!

❧ **75** ❧

Look what the town holds,
The journey of life it unfolds.
From Silence to chaos,
And chaos to silence— there is only loss!
The touching breeze of the sisters bazaar,
The lost business of Landour bazaar.
From The chaotic Mall road,
To the silence of the Landour—
Look and see deeply
The journey of life that the Queen presents.
The world is here,
The heart is here.
Just a few needs,
And everything is here.
We are all a traveller
From the chaos,
Seeking solace in the Queen
Somehow!

❧ 76 ❧

I know not what holds the fate,
And today nothing is the same.
Look at the nature,
Fading traces of the creator!
Voices unheard,
Even the chirping of the birds;
Hypocrisy at its peak,
Making the idea weak.
But who cares,
Realize, loyalty is so rare.
I've seen the town expanding
In reality, humans destroying.
If only we had reflected,
Things wouldn't have been fabricated.
Politics played in minor things here,
Why go further, when everything ends there.

77

It's in my town,
That politics exists everywhere.
The Queen isn't what it was,
She has seen the war.
But why has everything changed,
Fading beauty and history estranged!
Such a beautiful town,
Now burdened by politics.
A lot of sage!
But no body to rage.
Hearts endure,
Only to seek a cure;
No 'lover' hesitated
To leave the queen devastated.
I feel,
As the Queen has a lot to deal!
Landour has a lot to share,
If only the residents would care.

❧ 78 ❧

What about the values,
Destruction is what the people choose.
As seasons change,
An unknown feeling emerges;
The heart doesn't rage
As love tends to cease.
Where is that belongingness now?
Empty promises and empty vows.
Lost in dreams and utter silence,
Each one of us lack guidance;
A question emerges out of fear:
What if my town becomes a city?
Let it remain unanswered,
Sigh!

✹ 79 ✹

Hold the Queen's crown,
We'll save the town!
There is a blessing in being here,
Rising over the materialistic fear!
Prevailing compassion,
Humility is a passion!
A place blessed with possibilities,
Tourism testing abilities;
I know it's hard,
To stay away from your soil.
But no one cares
To preserve the queen's land.
No one thought,
The glory would be snatched!
In that monetary pursuits,
We've come far away from roots!

❧ **80** ❧

The freezing winters in my town,
The snow is all around.
But is everything the same now,
Or problems, we are welcoming now.
Tourists and traffic here,
For 'lovers' this is a problem mere.
The mountains covered with snow,
Never making you feel low.
For the people here,
Nature shows different colours.
But all this while, we ignore,
Until the nature roars
Landour longs,
Sings the songs.
People can change it,
Bit by bit!

81

Let me decide,
And go for a walk.
Find peace,
To let life go at ease.
Forget everything and heal,
From the chaos, let silence speak
Of the history of Sisters bazaar,
And the view of the landour bazaar.
Landour is God's own town,
The jewel on the Queen's crown!
Oh, the people of Landour,
Endure!
Take pride in its glory,
This isn't just a beautiful story.
A lot more is untold,
Hope destiny unfolds.

82

The crown has faded,
And maybe we are late
To understand its value—
Impressions of truth gives the clue
Of the Queen's glorious heritage,
And to the lost souls- we pay a homage.
Because of our past,
Proudly exists our present.
It is upon us to step back—
And revisit our lost heritage:
The fame of my Queen,
That has no longer been!

83

Glory did fade,
People left.
Lot more has changed,
Only memories are left.
People could do wonders,
But there were just blunders.
We've lost it all.
For the youth, it was a matter small.
Who valued our history,
The serenity turning mystery!
The silence leads to chaos,
And finally succumbing to greed.
How long should we hear the voice false?
Ignoring all that the Queen needs!
There's a lot more to my town,
For long, we have turned it down.

❧ **84** ❧

Walking and walking,
My heart still longing.
Longing to heal
The wounds of my Queen.
I had heard stories
Invoking the glories—
But one thing was told by my granny,
Change did arrive subtly!
The people of the queen's land.
Mere rumours they made grand:
And yet for peace they craved.
Look how they behaved!
We're all at fault,
A truth you won't like at all:
Let me clearly state:
We may pray—
To save the town:
But every hope ended the day,
You started abusing the crown.

85

My heart grieves,
When the pain of my Queen, it sees.
There is lost glory,
And greed further spoils this story.
The first-settlers of the town,
Preserved the crown!
Look at how the present choose to tease—
Destroying even the peace.
And silence is fading
As the cars are hovering,
And hearts are breaking-
To find the traces disappearing;
Even the efforts are lost,
Nothing much to sort.
No respite was seen,
They were resolved to hurt the Queen!
But don't tell anyone,
How change was used as a weapon.
As I write the untold,
Hope truth unfolds.

86

The Queen epitomizes life,
As the residents strive;
From the powerful silence
Of the Sisters bazaar,
Through the often found chaos
Of the Landour Bazaar—
Finally reaching the silence
Of the Happy Valley now.
The mall road's avidity
Adding to Queen's beauty!
But will we ever
Value this beautiful town?
The forefathers of the town,
You would've seen them frown,
To see things changing,
People migrating!
Oh! How painful it is to leave
A story in-between;
The change is brought to deceive,
Shattering every dream!

❦ **87** ❦

The arrival of the winters,
Bringing along the numbness—
The queen drenched in snow,
And as you know-
It looks as if the nature sympathizes,
As the beauty mesmerizes.
The winters too cold,
And bliss it holds!
It is a prelude to the revival
Of Nature and Queen's survival;
The crowd enters the town,
The hopes, it never lets down.
The snow and Silence,
Making the town look pious.
The beautiful views,
Giving us clues
Of the world and life,
Reminding that beauty never dies.

88

Some winters come late,
Abiding by their fate;
Bask as long as the sun shines
And write as long as the words rhyme!
When nature is celebrated no more,
Don't ask for a cure:
Choose to step away
Instead of living here at bay!
And as the schools shut down
To give way to the snowy days,
Notice how the nature amuses—
Giving birth to majestic views,
Then, you'll find people
Sitting beside the fireplace
Seeking warmth
Until the month of March,
Until the winters fade out!

89

A new beginning round the corner,
Everyone waits for days warmer;
Springs rejuvenates the Queen—
Look how the Buransh blooms
Breaking the gloom—
An air of joy blows,
Admire and let words flow!
See the blessing that we've received,
With hopes, a dream was conceived—
Despite the shallow narrations,
Unexpected desperations,
Seek what a lover would in reality mean—
Rise above the myopic greed,
Choose what the town needs.

90

Springs bring along hope,
And tourists from around the world—
The Queen welcomes warmly,
Embracing them entirely;
And while the crowd is around,
Cheerfulness surrounds.
Engaging with the history,
Reaffirming the glory of the town.
Limits should be respected,
Before it is time to be corrected!
But blinded by the greed,
None pays the heed—
And leave the Queen suffering,
You and me— longing!

91

Hot summers embrace the town,
You see the traffic up and down;
But summers weren't always so cruel,
We know the ones responsible!
Seasons are changing,
As if the cold wind blowing;
Tourists— more and more,
Why should one be filled with remorse!
The love for my Queen in our eyes—
Inspire others to call her a paradise!
But all this comes with pain too,
Scarcity of water and tanks to and fro!
And there some people repairing their roofs,
Before the rains profuse.
But summers hardly stay,
Have you ever heard the nature betray?
We've let ourselves fall,
And yet fail to recall.

92

Scorching heat,
But passion it never beats.
People working hard everyday,
To earn a living and happily stay!
Children playing and shouting
Elders on a long walk in the evening—
I see the Queen's guests
Coming to heal themselves.
The locals cherishing their precious time,
And with teary eyes, bidding good bye.
Somewhere the clouds have always been,
Bringing some relief now.
And everyone is seen
Going for walks now.
Evening time brings bustle,
Cool winds make it divine.

93

Touched by the drops of rain now,
Monsoons arrive in full form.
The clouds and the mist,
Rains settling the dust!
Sisters bazaar embraced by the fog,
You may also find some enthusiasts jog;
Landour is heavenly,
As the wind and rains align—
To adorn this beautiful place of mine—
The sun and clouds acting playfully
Mornings begin with light rains,
Bringing along the fog again!
Relieving the Queen from summer's pain,
And look what remains:
Clouds leave artistic traces
Inexpressible in phrases!

❧ **94** ❧

Only my heart knows,
Of the pain that I feel,
Of the talks that I hear
About the beauty that faded;
But who is to be blamed,
For its we who have lived here.
Understand— how our politics
Carries grave danger today.
Just feel the breeze,
And you'll hear words deep.
That some things weren't meant to change,
Tell me, how many of us even care.
She's called the Queen of hills,
But do we treat her as a Queen.
Today, our Queen is in pain,
Something no words can explain!

95

Clear skies,
Let the heart try
To heal the wounds of my town,
Seasons change then and now!
Autumns keep the question living:
Will the people ever strive
To make Landour better?
A place that was green,
Where beauty was real indeed.
The poet is helpless,
Even the words are useless.
But the heart knows,
To whomsoever it goes,
The response will make it weak,
Answer me, if you can:
How can one sit and stare
At the town's fading legacy,
Our Queen losing glory!

 96

Clouds cry,
Sigh!
The rains beautify,
Let no one lie.
Clouds all around,
Petrichor surrounds;
The town is blessed,
But rains too create a mess.
Though a cycle of nature,
It seems an answer to Queen's prayers!
Blessed with greenery,
Nature paints scenery!
But where does Landour,
Gets lost midway;
Tell me frankly,
Has landour become an alley?

❧ 97 ❧

Autumns divine,
Hear me tonight!
Look at the history the Queen bears!
We only need to care.
Before it fades,
To see there's nothing in the shades,
Landour takes form in the charm
To see the winter line form.
But is anybody concerned?
Why is the Queen left cornered?
History isn't bound to lose,
Let's turn it into a muse
For the generations to come,
And feel the pride that is!
Landour isn't lost, however,
Rise and care for ever!

98

Beauty lies everywhere,
But who is willing to see it.
Mussoorie isn't just a place,
It's a paradise for eternity.
Are we grateful?
Are we careful?
For generations, the town bloomed,
Uncountable people settled!
But see the plight of Landour,
It longs for a cure!
And so I'll write
Till the very end and rage.
I'll wait for the sight—
People will rise and engage!

99

The town waits,
For the winterline rare.
But how many of us care
To watch this sight so pleasant,
Nature's scenic beauty
That makes me poetically state!
The people of the town here,
Don't give heed now.
Landour is disturbed,
It seems always ignored.
And this walking away from heritage,
Should invite strong rage!
For my town, I am writing,
For many won't be liking.
Politics harmed the Queen, no doubt!
Only for votes, they shout!

❧ **100** ❧

Curse on Landour or on its people?
Will we never see it prosper.
Whenever a voice is raised,
They know how to suppress it there.
Our ancestors must be crying above,
The town that they had settled with love!
The town that saved lives—
Now longs for a life!
I know not how you may take it,
But the young should remember it.
The way this heart is writing this,
All I hope to be a witness
To the deeds that may bring back the glory,
And not become a forgotten story!
Save the Queen,
Listen to the Queen!

❧ **101** ❧

My heart longs
To find the problem that exists—
Every act is selfish—
Every act has intentions for politics.
Votes play an important role,
In selling my Queen's soul.
Every voice is shut here,
So no one would dare!
The beacon of hope new,
Dies every time, we get to view
The same story repeating again,
And love for our town is impacted again.
Emotions won't deceive!
And if you don't wish to believe—
Choose to look back at the past,
Your love for Queen will last!

❧ 102 ❧

What if we have truly failed,
Nothing much we have gained
From our indifferences,
Nothing we could strive;
And through this silence,
How would the parasites survive?
Showing no support to one another,
A lobby survives to bother!
I am of no view
But when realization strikes a few—
You'll find Landour surviving,
The Queen longing
To reclaim the lost glory,
And no longer worry!

✤ 103 ✤

Landour sleeps,
The Queen weeps;
What if the town is lost,
Will we never understand?
I can see ignorance,
Towards my Landour—
Heritage has destroyed,
Traditions changed.
But when the elders are nostalgic,
With sadness, I sense the fall!
Lives changed,
Times changed.
But hope keeps us alive—
Hope of timelessness of our Queen!
It is our legacy without a doubt
That we have truly lost.

❧ 104 ❧

Too many expert advices,
None to speak for the town.
They speak where they find
Monetary benefit they can bind!
I'll hold my words,
For I know, they don't know more.
I've seen them on a holiday trip,
Visiting and posting things.
But who cares really?
Hypocrisy is what makes them fairy.
Landour isn't Lost,
For heritage lies gloriously here.
The youth isn't Lost,
For lovers still live here.
But then what is lost,
Existence of the town?

105

Schools make the Queen proud,
Let's tell it loud.
Schools have tag,
Don't turn it rag.
Keep politics away from it,
Or else face the consequences.
Hold on and talk,
And let's go for a walk.
I've felt the need,
For universities, no one pays heed.
And see what do we lack,
Introspection is too rare.
Will they ever understand,
How separation from your birthplace
Isn't a pride to carry on your sleeves,
But a curse for those who believe!

❧ **106** ❧

Landour my town,
Look how much it costs
To shelter the people somehow,
Giving life anyhow!
Since ages,
The Queen has escaped changes!
With villagers from nearby
Adding vigor to the life here!
Mussoorie has strongly stood
Despite being at times shook!
For the harmony is unique,
The hills can't turn bleak;
We need to inculcate
The love that I hereby state:
The world admires our Queen's beauty,
And it is our wholesome duty
To preserve what is left
And beware of the cultural theft!

❧ 107 ❧

I've yearned,
I've learned.
For years living here,
It is silence that I have searched.
Where has Landour lost,
Like the glory of Mussoorie.
But people around,
Unknown to the glorious history for now.
The Queen is incomplete
Without Landour's narrow streets!
Did you care about the soul:
That now is fighting for an existence—
What else shall be the goal
Of so much reluctance?
Repeat— speak aloud:
Landour won't be lost.

❧ 108 ☙

This is much like an ode,
As the senior citizens behold.
Oh! You all are a strength of our town,
Don't let your voices go down.
Each one special,
Each one unique.
You preserve the foundation,
Of this hill station.
You solely hold the vision
To see through the treachery
Your wrinkles have seen the crown—
The glorious heritage of the town.
You've kept the hope alive,
Giving us reason to strive:
For gratitude, words aren't enough,
You've seen it all- the smooth and the rough!

🌿 109 🌿

Tell me, haven't we lost
The heritage of the town,
Do we understand the cost?
Of stealing the Queen's crown!
I see people running away
And not letting the town grow;
The only way is to pray—
As emotions overflow;
The young looking for universities-
Seeking opportunities!
Queen's fame solely doesn't help,
Real problem can't be suppress;
Youth in politics is a trend here,
Ending up as an instrument mere!
Not a word is spoken,
None is awaken!

✦ 110 ✦

Come, look at the festive celebrations,
Driving off the frustration;
See as we together celebrate,
Essence of unity we thereby state.
Yes, the town is rapidly changing,
Rituals and traditions succumbing-
Aren't we responsible?
Who else is accountable?
The young needs to understand,
This is the time to take a stand
For the lost culture and traditions,
Left only in a few renditions;
Often you'll hear them say:
"Now nothing is the same,"
And then with hope they pray,
But no one they blame.

❧ **111** ❧

Mullingar bears history,
Notice its trajectory—
First residence in the town,
Mullingar was Queen's crown!
No relevance is seen now,
If only the lovers saw—
The place where history was made—
And today I am afraid-
There is but silence around—
Only buildings surround;
Who really cares?
There are but tears—
Why is my Landour neglected?
Why is the Queen misunderstood!
From childhood I've seen,
Very few are keen
On preserving the glory
From being inscribed in forgotten history.

112

Look at how the Queen has cared,
Our future she has prepared—
The schools have blessed us all,
With gratitude we all should recall;
It may be late,
To know what states the fate-
But an awakening is a boon
That must happen soon:
She is a sage:
Embodiment of the river of knowledge,
And this truth must be respected,
Not lamented;
The Queen has created visionaries,
Let us respect our history!

❧ 113 ❧

The Queen is hopeful,
Often she is grateful.
But there occurs events strange
Evidence of how times change!
Landour ignored every time,
And with sadness I write.
Landour's story has lessons
For the ones willing to listen—
Carrying an urge not to part,
Purest emotions of the heart:
But will people ever be grateful?
Is it enough to be hopeful?
Emerging from doon valley,
It is hope that I carry!

❦ 114 ❦

Landour, you've never been bound—
But blessed by people around,
With hearts so pure,
The elders relate to a fruitful tenure
Of the selfless lovers of the town—
Who cared for the Queen's crown!
The legacy lives with us,
Carrying it gently is a must.
The feeling that thus surrounds,
Echoes of the love that has been around;
The British-era houses still stand
Unlike the grains of sand!
What if nothing was meant to die,
But left for us to learn and sigh—
If only we could try—
My Queen wouldn't have to cry;
Over the loss of the town old,
Let the pain in words unfold!

❦ 115 ❦

When hope fades quietly,
And every urge vanishes subtly,
See the materialists wonder
Of how the lovers never surrender;
Feel the Queen,
And what her longing means,
Seek the magnificence of the sky
Understand the meaning behind the sigh!
Time for benediction,
To be blessed with an unwavering conviction—
We have lived for her,
And shall die for the same!
Our words won't just resonate here,
But shall echo until we reclaim!
A thousand feelings rise,
With tears in eyes—
Longing for the heritage,
Before it is late!

116

Silence takes over,
Voices lost forever.
The light fades,
Now see what remains:
Darkness profound
In the town renowned—
Two hundred years passed,
Only to be harassed;
Nothing left for the choices,
Cries and unheard Voices.
Nature reminds,
But who would care to mind—
No feelings respected,
Demands neglected.
I speak for my town— clearly,
I carry hopes sincerely!

117

A prayer for my lifeline,
So the spirit shouldn't die-
And even they try to destroy that,
We'll cling on to past:
Concrete structures everywhere,
And pages of history they tear;
I may lament-
But everything is now of cement!
Nature has herself hidden
As if presence is forbidden—
Landour has lost the charm,
Nothing more left to harm—
The villages around,
Adding pride to our town.
The bond among the residents,
Setting a precedence!

118

I've known the town,
The railway tracks on ground—
A dream incomplete,
A few still plead;
Why can't we take that forth,
The project of worth,
Yes, I know the town,
Since that electric bulb was lit,
Do we remember a bit?
Why did that love die?
I belong to a town,
That still is unexplored;
That still is so loving,
To hope I'm clinging.
The Queen knows me too,
She believes in the hope anew!

❧ 119 ❧

Lack of trust,
The Queen in stress,
In words deep I dive
Finding hope to survive:
It has been about existence-
To elude from repentance:
The trees can speak,
As the Queen gets weak;
Heritage has been here,
Landour isn't an area mere.
In the laps of the Queen,
Lives have changed,
What was meant to be serene,
Has now turned strange—
But I know even when I fall,
For her lap, I'll make a loud call!

❧ 120 ❧

Gateway to the mighty himalayas,
Carrying hope for a million—
Is tourism the last straw,
Nothing else I saw;
We aren't losing the way,
But cautious we must stay.
Myopic minds won't give ease—
See as they temporarily appease.
We have to let it go
Before it is late.
You may go with the flow,
But dare to state:
The tragedy that has befallen,
The history before it is forgotten!

121

Of the changes I hear.
Tell me, is this fare?
The town isn't the same
From what it was a decade ago:
But one has to introspect,
Should we call this town perfect?
Of course, there are problems today,
Blame politics as much as you may—
They are politically divided,
But for Mussoorie, they must be united,
After creating a mess,
It seems they're all heartless;
And let me tell it loud,
If they'll be allowed,
You'll see Landour suffering all the more,
And a dearth of a cure!

122

Inheritance we took for granted,
For identity, my Landour confronted—
It has longed for years,
Amidst infinite tears.
The pain of Landour,
Has been left unsaid.
For people don't understand,
And no one is willing to take a stand,
Shops are closing,
As if everything eluding-
The idea of togetherness exists no more,
Yet I wish to restore
Everything that I've seen fading
Away from the laps of Landour.
Who would like to see this fall,
Will you ever recall?

❦ 123 ❦

Those days of Landour,
When cars weren't allowed.
When roads were clean,
And the residents had a reason to feel proud!
Where are the deodar trees?
Where are the sparrows?
Where are the basket pullers-
And rickshaws that moved on the roads.
Lost is the rickshaw stand,
Baskets, palanquin and Prams.
Pollution free was our town,
Too much shine was there in the crown—
Peaceful and quiet,
Showcasing Queen's might.

🌿 124 🌿

This is a beautiful place,
The poets long to embrace;
I can hear the children on the swings,
And happiness the evening brings!
The villagers returning home,
And find their horses that roam,
There isn't any horse-stand
But who cares to demand!
A lot has changed in Landour,
And this isn't an evening hour—
Hope we cannot lose,
Let evenings turn into muse.
Those who felt the change,
Would relate and rage,
And those who have not-
Should give it a thought.

⚘ 125 ⚘

In the town, I live,
I long and sing
The melodies of heritage,
Of memories and of change;
It's tough to hold-
Only to see longings go untold-
No tears can wash them—
The feelings that go numb,
A glorious history
Almost into dust now.
The hills and the birds,
Long for their eternal song.
The change does hurt,
As nostalgia takes birth,
And no sight of accountability,
Tends to mark the severity.

❧ 126 ❧

The captivating landscapes,
Inspiring you and me to escape
Only to watch the scenic view,
And wish: some places no one knew!
There is a touch of nature here,
Something too rare—
In the woods, we find our way,
Evenings bring some moments to pray—
But the pain isn't unknown,
Life goes on with what fate has shown,
Our love for the town,
Doesn't give us the moment to frown.
Years ago we felt lively,
Decisions were taken wisely,
There was a natural connection,
Bearing impressions of pure intention.

127

How long should I wait?
Is this my Queen's fate?
Hypocrisy is visible,
Making lives miserable—
As originality is lost,
Chaos is present of all sorts;
This place isn't same anymore,
Come, sit and stare—
A common feeling we share,
Unknown to the cure!
You and I have no say,
So the parasites choose their way
And ruin the town slowly,
As we watch closely,
Words— watch as they touch hearts,
A revival would thereby start!

128

Never forget your roots,
Reflect in them your boons—
When a town is found,
A civilization is born.
A culture that grows,
Through highs and lows—
We are but an outcome,
My Queen blessing each one,
So that hope prevails,
And no one fails
To feel the pride in where we are,
To feel the pride in who we are.
Time to realize this,
Don't give it a miss-
What has been the charm,
Remember not to harm!

❧ 129 ❧

Chilled winters and no snow,
Even as the temperature is low.
There was a time in history,
It snowed in abundance-
And now there is no clarity,
Just some hope for repentance—
Concrete buildings high!
Sight brings Sigh!
The curse of pollution that was given,
Degrading of nature unforbidden.
Snowy mountains – a rare scene,
Know what this may mean:
Time is less- realize
Don't limit yourself to the sighs!
Longings are not wrong,
Time for us to rewrite the eternal song!

130

See how the wrong steps were taken,
And people remained silent.
My Queen numb,
The lovers not willing to succumb;
I look for words that are present,
Affinity inspires us to resent-
For they emerge from the heart,
Only a few things that last.
The buildings – our heritage lie in silence,
Rare to see any resilience.
Lost is the glory of the my town,
No one cares for the Queen's crown:
Even the trees feel the pain,
While the soil has nothing to gain.
Hold the tears
That carry longings of years!

131

Purpose of our birth,
On a place called heaven on earth.
Realization isn't in the mirth,
Of seekers there is a dearth.
Longing for the eternity,
A place of bliss and serenity.
The bond that has been lost,
No one enquires about the cost!
Landour echoes
And there blooms the roses,
The land bearing unprecedented past,
Will the glory last?
A touching sight of liveliness,
Giving way to peacefulness.
Cherish before it is lost,
Realize before it gets lost!

132

Indebted to this land,
An answer you and I demand,
A hope that the change
Would pacify the rage-
But change is brutal—
Validated by people cruel;
You and me watch it all,
Certain about the fall—
There is a hope somewhere,
Giving me a reason rare,
Words will show the way,
Landour will rise one day.
The hope that brings us close,
A fight none should lose!
As realizations occur,
The Queen should prosper.

133

Landour longs
For the season of happiness,
For the good old days
Of life and hopefulness.
The mesmerizing springs,
When you could hear the birds sing—
The melodies of hope for tomorrow,
Transcending Landour's sorrow;
Nothing left for lamentation,
Preserve the town with no hesitation-
The legacy of Landour is in our hands,
Make sure our love withstands,
For this place is eternal,
And our love not ephemeral-
Understand,
Time to take a stand.

❦ 134 ❦

The trails of our past,
Asserting that the glory should last—
The Kipling trail guides us along,
It is here the nature and us belong;
The History can't be forgotten,
And not everything has to be rewritten,
Look at everything we have to handle,
Preserve the history from getting dismantle.
The trail holds our history,
Especially for those who wish to travel daily-
The trail that led to the Queen,
And there began an eternal tale-
Striving through the hatred in disguise,
The boons too have come as a surprise.
This trail is indelible,
Like an impression poetical!

135

Our Queen had her own Koh-i-noor,
Adding to the glory all the more—
That today is abandoned, broken,
Inculcating painful emotions unspoken.
Kohinoor of our Landour,
Had an unsparing struggle to endure,
Was all this a must?
Enough to destabilize the trust!
Look at the path of our town,
Majestic realms they swear to bring down.
The evolution of time does signify,
The nature's call of the day.
Before we sleep tonight,
Ensure the Queen rises- against the time!

Odes

Expressions Of Gratitude.

Ode To Ancestors

Looking from where I am,
I see everything as a sham
Except the legacy
That becomes a cherished melody!
Those were the days
When humility bloomed
At every gaze
And the blessing wasn't abused;
But I did realize
From the hopeless sigh—
Everything that was
And everything that is
Holds no eternal relevance
For people drenched in negligence!
Where is their hope that existed
In the unity of the town?
What if their dreams had ignited
The urge to save the Queen's crown!
But here I am— reminiscing,
At the past I'm fondly looking;
Honouring the golden time,
And succumbing to what is destined!

Ode To Mother Ganga

The river holding us,
A message of life, it gives us.
Flow, keep flowing like her,
Have you seen her stopping ever?
She saw the world changing,
Lives slowly ageing.
Satisfying the needs of all,
For humanity's sake, she is serving all.
Grateful for what you have done,
Like a mother, taken care of us.
You are the eternal—
Your flow cleansing the mind.
Inspiring lives,
Encouraging us to strive:
Blessing the civilization,
Endorsing realizations.

Reflection

We all, at some point of time, long for peace, for love and for understanding. Here, the longings hold a message for its readers. The past that seems to be forgotten and the past that has been taken for granted longs for revival. Landour has been a witness to the fast changing times. It has seen people growing and evolving with time. Landour has seen people coming and going, migrating and many people from different villages settling down here. The heart of Landour is so big that it welcomed people from all walks of life, from different places around the world. The legacy of Landour can be traced from the places where British relics still exist and that reflects upon the lives and the everlasting history. Longings are an appeal to refrain from erasing the past or break the past. Somewhere, we as citizens of Landour and Mussoorie have failed to keep and preserve the legacy. Earlier there used to less number of shops and from everywhere you could have glimpse of the natural beauty but sadly these things are rare now. The way Landour has evolved with concrete structures, even breathing fresh air is difficult at times..

Landour is the heart of Mussoorie. While I go for a walk from sister's bazaar down to the Landour market, I miss a lot of things here. I miss those people, some trees. I miss those places where people used to sit and chat. I miss those places where I could feel the relaxing vibes of the town. I miss those silent, cheerful evenings as people have left their homeland to earn their living. I miss the young playing on the grounds. I miss people going for walks. I miss those people who carried the feeling of oneness and lived in Landour. I miss the culture that existed. The way the people of Jaunpur and Jaunsar feel proud of their culture and live it every moment is a source of inspiration for all. The traditions, the rituals and the cultural heritage and legacy they carry reflect their connection with the roots and that one should never forget the roots.

I don't say that rejuvenation is bad but the legacy should be kept in mind. Snowfall is slowly becoming a rare sight now. When I get to hear history from people and they relate to the amount and the time period of snowfall, it brings so much pain. We are doers, we are the future. It lies not just on the stakeholders but on each and everyone living in Mussoorie to understand. Landour has suffered a lot but Mussoorie should not walk on the same path. Landour has seen the toughest times and sought opportunities. The heritage of Landour needs to be preserved and protected. Landour holds nostalgia of the golden days. Sadly, migration has changed a lot in Landour. People migrate to doon valley in search of employment opportunities and so on. No one wants to leave their homeland or their birthplace but for jobs they have to do so. The stakeholders of Mussoorie should aim at improving and establishing employment opportunities that will help the town grow. Self-employment should be the aim of the people.

In the changing times, we have to look at the concept of sustainable development. We have to think not just for today but for tomorrow as well. Landour should be declared as the heritage zone of Mussoorie. Mussoorie has been losing its glory from past 10-15 years. What is fading today is the real Landour. What is fading today is the feeling that existed in Landour among the people. What is fading is the hope to see a new morning of good changes in the town.

The poems have clearly aimed at the hopes that may pave a new way for the town. It is the legacy that is spoken of. Demographic changes are taking place rapidly in Mussoorie. There is a threat to the cultural legacy and the cultural heritage. The people, especially the youth is moving out of their homeland in search of a living and once they go out, they cannot/ don't want to come back. It's just their helplessness that make them migrate to different parts of the country. Sadly they have to leave their families to earn a living. The glory for which Landour and Mussoorie were famous- are fading today. Youth is migrating from the Queen of Hills. The past has been forgotten by people. The journey of life never stops in Landour. In a world of utter turbulences and inevitable circumstances, Mussoorie gives us the refuge and support and surely, the place, the land, the people will continue to inspire, lead, give refuge, support and understand people. It's time we take the beauty of our legacy, the land, the culture and the people of mussoorie to the world.

While we grow, we should not forget our roots and our connection with it. No matter which direction the branches or the shoots grow up, one must always be proud of where one comes from. One must always be directed towards making the Queen and Landour proud in as many ways as one can. Landour has lived and seen the journey, it has lived in lives, it has felt lives. Landour has been a boon to the people in many ways. It is said that the things we don't value gets lost in time so therefore, we have to realize and start valuing the land, the Queen which has given us so many things, so many memories. It's the need of an hour that heritage and legacy needs to be kept in mind. It's the legacy that holds us and it's through the legacy, our existence is justified. We are known by the Queen and we are because of the Queen.

For the sake of our town,

This book has been written for the sake of our town. With the demographic changes taking place and migration at its peak, it becomes necessary to revisit the past and establish a connection with the town that was once full of glory and life. For the sake of our town, I can't see it in pain. The degradation of land and nature is visible to each one of us. For the sake of our town, we'll write. The traditions are no where to be seen. The way the town has changed drastically is concerning. Every time the wind blows, it makes us ponder on how time has changed, how our town has changed. It makes us realise that how our town 'has been' ruined with time. For the sake of our town, we all have to look into how we can give our best for preserving the town. How can we contribute to the sustainable development of my town. How can we stop migration from the town and in the hills and move towards self-reliance.

I wrote for the sake of my town,
We wrote for the sake of our town.
Long live my town!

For The Sake Of Our Town!